Bond

CW01676517

Verbal Reasoning

10 Minute Tests

9–10 years

OXFORD
UNIVERSITY PRESS

Test 1: Similars and Opposites

Test time: 0 5 10 minutes

Underline the two words in each line which are most similar in type or meaning.

Example	<u>dear</u>	pleasant	poor	extravagant	<u>expensive</u>
1	flexible	rigid	stiff	friendly	clever
2	table	mirror	basin	door	bath
3	apple	pear	carrot	rose	nettle
4	busy	clear	stormy	quick	obvious
5	lorry	aeroplane	boat	yacht	train

Underline the two words, one from each group, which are the most opposite in meaning.

Example	(dawn, <u>early</u>, wake)	(<u>late</u>, stop, sunrise)
6	(tidy, burn, flame)	(neat, messy, fire)
7	(house, soft, concrete)	(hard, cement, stable)
8	(right, river, solid)	(liquid, rigid, water)
9	(confident, timid, bashful)	(careful, tearful, shy)
10	(high, over, beside)	(through, under, above)

Underline the pair of words most similar in meaning.

Example	come, go	<u>roam, wander</u>	fear, fare
11	half, crumb	complete, whole	right, wrong
12	grip, clasp	release, hold	balance, fall
13	answer, question	repair, spoil	problem, difficulty
14	appear, arrive	come, go	disappear, return
15	warm, cool	climb, drop	feel, touch

Underline the word in brackets that is most opposite in meaning to the word in capitals.

Example	WIDE	(broad	vague	long	<u>narrow</u>	motorway)
16	GIVE	(present	grant	result	spare	take)
17	FLAT	(house	even	odd	bumpy	high)
18	BELOW	(under	above	on	beneath	between)
19	SHINY	(dull	quick	cloud	metal	sum)
20	END	(corner	side	beginning	middle	top)

Total

TEST 2: Sorting Words 1

Test time: 0 5 10 minutes

Underline the one word in the brackets which will go equally well with both the pairs of words outside the brackets.

Example	rush, attack	cost, fee	(price, hasten, strike, <u>charge</u>, money)
1	leave, separate	piece, share	(bit, portion, part, holiday, section)
2	beat, punch	success, achievement	(hit, smack, purpose, thump, give)
3	box, case	stem, torso	(tree, trunk, luggage, suitcase, body)
4	shiny, glowing	clever, intelligent	(dull, light, bright, smart, quick)
5	dig, sow	tree, bush	(leaf, vegetable, spade, rake, plant)

Underline the two words which are the odd ones out in the following groups of words.

Example	black	<u>king</u>	purple	green	<u>house</u>
6	shirt	vest	socks	shoes	trousers
7	ferry	bicycle	yacht	skateboard	windsurfer
8	eyes	hat	nose	mouth	glove
9	middle	edge	bottom	border	side
10	safe	secure	sausage	sound	sick

Rearrange the muddled letters in capitals to make a proper word. The answer will complete the sentence sensibly.

Example A BEZAR is an animal with stripes. ZEBRA

11 Two TNNIOCNTES of the world are Africa and Asia. ________

12 The storm brought down an ECLETRCI cable. ________

13 Don't forget to lock the RTOFN door! ________

14 We are going to the ASEDIES on Saturday if it is sunny. ________

15 Sarah loves ice cream with COHCOTELA sauce. ________

Find and underline the two words which need to change places for the sentence to make sense.

Example She went to <u>letter</u> the <u>write</u>.

16 Dairy give us cows products.

17 Number other is on the twenty side of the street.

18 Some were given you homework.

19 Can you close door the please?

20 My red is blue and shirt.

Total

TEST 3: Sorting Words 2

Test time: 0 5 10 minutes

Add one letter to the word in capital letters to make a new word. The meaning of the new word is given in the clue.

Example	PLAN	simple	plain
1	HAIR	seat	______
2	SPED	pay out	______
3	ROOF	evidence	______
4	SALLOW	not deep	______
5	HEEL	car part	______

Find a word that is similar in meaning to the word in capital letters and that rhymes with the second word.

Example	CABLE	tyre	wire
6	FOOTWEAR	two	______
7	MASTER	sword	______
8	NARRATE	smell	______
9	MOULDY	mail	______
10	SHATTER	take	______

Underline the two words that are made from the same letters.

Example	TAP	PET	TEA	POT	EAT
11	DANCE	LANCE	LANES	CRANE	CLEAN
12	SLOPE	POLES	POSTS	LEAPS	PEEPS
13	FLAIR	FIRES	RIFLE	FRAIL	ROOFS
14	SWIRL	LOWER	WINGS	SWING	GRINS
15	LEAST	LASTS	STOOL	SLIPS	TALES

Rearrange the letters in capitals to make another word. The new word has something to do with the first two words.

Example	spot	soil	SAINT	STAIN
16	chair	bench	TEAS	______
17	bound	jump	PALE	______
18	cord	string	PORE	______
19	fall	drip	PROD	______
20	instruct	train	CHEAT	______

Total

Test 4: Selecting Words

Test time: 0 5 10 minutes

Underline two words, one from each group, that go together to form a new word. The word in the first group always comes first.

Example (hand, green, for) (light, house, sure)

1	(hand, foot, way)	(signal, path, shoe)
2	(green, apple, wood)	(picker, leaf, land)
3	(straw, hay, pink)	(berry, cloud, stick)
4	(old, bald, handy)	(horse, tyre, man)
5	(white, blue, clean)	(bath, wash, sky)

Find the letter which will end the first word and start the second word.

Example peac (h) ome

6 pla (___) ard

7 thin (___) ing

8 blu (___) yes

9 fou (___) eal

10 flo (___) ind

Complete the following sentences by selecting the most sensible word from each group of words given in the brackets. Underline the word selected.

Example The (children, boxes, foxes) carried) the (houses, books, steps) home from the (greengrocer, library).

11 Michael picked up the (oars, rubbish, pigeon) and expertly (climbed, talked, rowed) the boat to the (castle, shore, school).

12 The (rocket, train, promise) blasted into the (sky, rails, room) from the space (station, town, letter).

13 Mrs Patel (dropped, carried, drove) her car (under, into, between) the parking space and (sped, cleaned, turned) off the engine.

14 My (uncle, aunt, dog) Trevor is my (pet's, mother's, desk's) (chair, brother, wall).

15 Mr Bowen bent (up, down, along) to smell the (fragrant, cold, easy) rose in his (garden, bathroom, cupboard).

Underline the one word which cannot be made from the letters of the word in capital letters.

Example	STATIONERY	stone	tyres	ration	nation	noisy
16	RAINSTORM	stain	month	train	mains	roast
17	FAVOURABLE	blare	flour	brave	flavour	bluff
18	MARGARINE	argue	grain	margin	grime	enigma
19	HINDQUARTERS	quart	trend	strand	quince	trade
20	CRISPBREAD	price	pears	brisk	drape	pride

Total

TEST 5: Finding Words

Test time: 0 5 10 minutes

Find the four-letter word hidden at the end of one word and the beginning of the next word. The order of the letters may not be changed.

Example The children had bats and balls. sand

1. Please wait for me. ______
2. Your football team is good this season. ______
3. Jane painted her room peach and cream. ______
4. I need to remember to lock the front door. ______
5. Please stick the label to your jacket. ______

Find the three-letter word which can be added to the letters in capitals to make a new word. The new word will complete the sentence sensibly.

Example The cat sprang onto the MO. USE

6. She has grown her H long. ______
7. We went to France for our HOLI. ______
8. The village shop S at six o'clock yesterday. ______
9. The ambulance RUD the sick person to hospital. ______
10. Every morning Luke eats a B of cereal. ______

Find a word that can be put in front of each of the following words to make new, compound words.

Example	cast	fall	ward	pour	down
11	berry	board	currant	bird	______
12	cuff	bag	rail	shake	______
13	pot	spoon	cake	time	______
14	stairs	stream	standing	roar	______
15	boat	buoy	span	less	______

Move one letter from the first word and add it to the second word to make two new words.

Example	hunt	sip	hut	snip
16	fair	way	______	______
17	march	cob	______	______
18	every	early	______	______
19	teach	flee	______	______
20	climb	path	______	______

Total

TEST 6: Alphabetical Order and Substitution

Test time: 0 5 10 minutes

Underline the word in each line that has its letters in alphabetical order.

1	flare	flour	floor	fable	feeds
2	hosts	hilly	hello	hares	hinge
3	apply	above	acorn	adept	after
4	badger	better	believe	begging	begins
5	dwell	dizzy	defrost	deity	dense

If these words were written backwards and then placed in alphabetical order, which word would come fifth? Underline your answer.

6	ladle	paddle	little	stile	female
7	garland	garage	gallant	galaxy	gadget
8	goodness	fairness	kindness	sadness	likeness
9	biscuit	racket	ticket	chariot	bucket
10	nears	bears	fears	rears	tears

If A = 13, B = 10, C = 8, D = 6 and E = 1, find the answers to the following calculations.

11 A − E = ______________

12 BD = ______________

13 (B − C) + D = ______________

14 C + D + E = ______________

15 (A − C) + D = ______________

If A = 2, B = 3, C = 5, D = 6 and E = 10, give the answer to each of these calculations as a letter.

16 E − C = ______________

17 B + A + C = ______________

18 D ÷ A = ______________

19 E − (B + C) = ______________

20 A × B = ______________

Total

TEST 7: Word Progressions

Test time: 0 5 10 minutes

Look at the first group of three words. The word in the middle has been made from the other two words. Complete the second group of three words in the same way, making a new word in the middle.

Example	PAIN	INTO	TOOK	ALSO	SOON	ONLY
1	FEES	SINK	INKY	POST	______	REEK
2	DEAR	ARCH	CHIP	MOST	______	ARMY
3	BOAT	OATS	PINS	PEAS	______	GOAT
4	GEAR	GOLF	WOLF	CROW	______	SLAM
5	PART	PANE	WINE	EXAM	______	KNIT

Change the first word into the last word, by changing one letter at a time and making a new, different word in the middle.

Example	CASE	CASH	LASH
6	BIRD	______	WIND
7	TASK	______	WALK
8	BELT	______	BALL
9	WING	______	SONG
10	FAME	______	FARM

Change the first word of the third pair in the same way as the other pairs to give a new word.

Example	bind, hind	bare, hare	but, hut
11	take, teak	mate, meat	sale, ______
12	list, silt	last, salt	left, ______
13	fate, rate	fake, rake	fail, ______
14	wind, find	wool, fool	wall, ______
15	tops, spot	leer, reel	keep, ______

Find the missing number by using the two numbers outside the brackets in the same way as the other sets of numbers.

Example	2 [8] 4	3 [18] 6	5 [25] 5
16	7 [15] 8	6 [9] 3	13 [__] 3
17	2 [1] 2	4 [2] 2	6 [__] 3
18	4 [8] 2	4 [12] 3	3 [__] 5
19	13 [2] 11	21 [9] 12	16 [__] 8
20	3 [9] 3	8 [16] 2	5 [__] 4

Total

TEST 8: Logic

Test time: 0 5 10 minutes

Read the statements and then underline two of the five options below that must be true.

1–2 'Some roofs are made of tiles. All houses have roofs.'

All roofs are made of tiles.
All houses have tiles.
Tiles are a type of roof covering.
Straw can be a roof covering.
A house needs a roof.

3–4 'The police help to keep us safe and catch criminals. Some police officers wear helmets.'

Police officers must wear helmets at all times.
Police officers often work in pairs.
Helmets may be part of a police officer's uniform.
People feel safer when there is less crime.
Police officers help to catch people who break the law.

In a pet shop there are 5 hutches in a row. A different rabbit is in each hutch. Work out, from the clues, where each rabbit belongs.

1	2	3	4	5

The black rabbit is next to the white rabbit with red eyes.
The floppy eared rabbit is in one of the end hutches.
The fat rabbit is not next to the brown and white rabbit, and it is further to the right than the floppy eared rabbit.
The brown and white rabbit is between the floppy eared rabbit and the white rabbit.

5–9 HUTCH 1 ____________ HUTCH 3 ____________ HUTCH 5 ____________
HUTCH 2 ____________ HUTCH 4 ____________

Sam and Otis play football.
Tom, Mike and Sam play rugby.
Bob, Mike and Ravi play football and cricket.
Everyone likes computer games except Ravi.

10 Who likes cricket and rugby? ____________

11 How many children like computer games? ____________

12 Who likes rugby but not football? ____________

13 How many children like football but not computer games? ____________

14 Who likes football and rugby but not cricket? ____________

Janet's bookshelves are divided into 6 areas. She keeps different items in each section. From the information below, work out what goes into each section.

A	B
C	D
E	F

The novels are directly above the reference books.
The novels are directly to the right of the CDs.
The photographs are directly to the left of the DVDs.
The DVDs are above the novels.
The CDs are higher than the school books but lower than the photos.

15–20 novels ____ reference books ____ CDs ____
school books ____ photographs ____ DVDs ____

Time for a break! Go to Puzzle Page 42

Total

TEST 9: Codes

Test time: 0 5 10 minutes

Here are the number codes for four words. Match the right code to the right word.

BEND	BIND	BOOK	KIND
6538	0138	6138	6440

1 BEND ________ 2 BIND ________

3 BOOK ________ 4 KIND ________

5 Using the same code, decode 8435. ________

Solve the problems by working out the codes.

6 If 7914 is the code for FOUR, what does 794 stand for? ________

7 If 5612 is the code for MACE, what does 1652 stand for? ________

8 If 9461 is the code for PORE, what does 6491 stand for? ________

9 If 4813 is the code for CART, what does 183 stand for? ________

10 If 6972 is the code for TAME, what does 726 stand for? ________

Solve the problems by working out the letter codes. The alphabet has been written out to help you.

A B C D E F G H I J K L M N O P Q R S T U V W X Y Z

Example In a code, SECOND is written as UGEQPF.
How would you write THIRD? VJKTF

11 In a code, BISCUIT is written as CJTDVJU. How would you write BITS? ________

12 In a code, STEAM is written as UVGCO. How would you write MAST? ________

13 In a code, BRING is written as CSJOH. How would you write BEEN? ________

14 In a code, WHITE is written as VGHSD. How would you write HEEL? ________

15 In a code, PRIME is written as NPGKC. How would you write FOUL? ________

16 In a code, DREAM is written as GUHDP. Decode PDGH. ________

17 In a code, BRAIN is written as FVEMR. Decode RIIH. ________

18 In a code, GRIME is written as FQHLD. Decode FDQL. ________

19 In a code, FLOUR is written as DJMSP. Decode BCCN. ________

20 In a code, DRESS is written as CQDRR. Decode AHSD. ________

Total

TEST 10: Sequences

Test time: 0 5 10 minutes

Choose two words, one from each set of brackets, to complete the sentence in the best way.

Example Smile is to happiness as (drink, tear, shout) is to (whisper, laugh, sorrow).

1 River is to water as (stream, vein, fridge) is to (cold, blood, kitchen).

2 Winter is to cold as (summer, spring, fire) is to (log, hot, sunshine).

Complete the following sentence in the best way by choosing one word from each set of brackets.

Example Tall is to (tree, short, colour) as narrow is to (thin, white, wide).

3 Fish is to (fingers, pond, gills) as man is to (car, lungs, dinner).

4 Begin is to (finish, start, continue) as end is to (rear, finish, bottom).

5 Pause is to (break, snap, claws) as halt is to (go, start, stop).

Fill in the missing letters and numbers. The alphabet has been written out to help you.

A B C D E F G H I J K L M N O P Q R S T U V W X Y Z

Example AB is to CD as PQ is to RS.

6 ZX is to YW as XV is to ____.

7 Ae is to Fj as Ko is to ____.

8 ST is to UV as WX is to ____.

9 P3 is to O5 as N7 is to ____.

10 HJ is to JL as LN is to ____.

Give the missing numbers and letters in the following sequences.

Example	2	4	6	8	10	12
11	24	20	16	12	8	____
12	6	7	9	____	16	21
13	5	____	13	17	21	25
14	101	202	____	404	505	606
15	15t	17t	19u	21u	____	25v

Give the missing letters in the following sequences. The alphabet has been written out to help you.

A B C D E F G H I J K L M N O P Q R S T U V W X Y Z

Example	CQ	DP	EQ	FP	GQ	HP
16	EK	GL	____	KN	MO	OP
17	MN	____	OR	PT	QV	RX
18	PQ	PR	____	QT	RU	RV
19	PZ	QX	PV	QT	PR	____
20	Gu	____	Is	Jr	Kq	Lp

Total

TEST 11: Mixed

Test time: 0 5 10 minutes

Rearrange the muddled letters in capitals to make a proper word. The answer will complete the sentence sensibly.

Example A BEZAR is an animal with stripes. ZEBRA

1 If I make mistakes with my pencil, I use my BURREB. ______

2 At the beach I play with my TECKUB and spade. ______

3 In AUJANYR the weather is likely to be cold. ______

4 A bee or wasp GNIST is painful. ______

5 If you light matches near petrol there will be an ELXOPSOIN. ______

6 At RITCHSMAS we sing carols. ______

Answer these questions. The alphabet has been written out to help you.

A B C D E F G H I J K L M N O P Q R S T U V W X Y Z

7 Put the letters in the word SPECIAL in alphabetical order. ______

8 Which is now the fifth letter? ______

9 Put the letters in the word PREACH in alphabetical order. ______

10 Which is now the fourth letter? ______

Find a word that is similar in meaning to the word in capital letters and that rhymes with the second word.

Example CABLE tyre wire

11 MARK mane ______

12 TERROR deer ______

13 SHOP moor ______

14 PRESERVE wave ______

15 WICKED while ______

Solve the problems by working out the codes.

16 If the code for FLAMES is SDQRPN, what is the code for SEAM? ______

17 If the code for BLAST is XNRFE, what is the code for STALL? ______

18 If the code for QUITE is 59432, what is the code for TIE? ______

19 If the code for TWIST is bxyzb, what is the code for SIT? ______

20 If the code for SLUMP is FTRXY, what is the code for PLUM? ______

Total

Test 12: Mixed

Test time: 0 5 10 minutes

If these words were listed in reverse alphabetical order, which word would come second?

1	brooch	break	bracken	bruise	bridge	______
2	chimney	choose	cherub	cheek	chapel	______
3	penguin	pedal	penny	peony	pecan	______
4	darkness	danger	dancing	dampen	dainty	______

Solve the problems by working out the codes.

5 If 8641 is the code for TEAS, what does 1648 stand for? ______

6 If 3996 is the code for GOOD, what does 693 stand for? ______

7 If 6752 is the code for MITE, what does 5762 stand for? ______

8 If 8491 stands for GRAB, what does 194 stand for? ______

Complete the following expressions by filling in the missing word.

Example Pen is to ink as brush is to paint.

9 Kennel is to dog as stable is to ______.

10 Cushion is to chair as pillow is to ______.

11 Butterfly is to six legs as bird is to ______ legs.

12 Picture is to wall as rug is to ______.

Town A is directly north of Town B.
Town C is west of B but south of D.
If the towns make a square on a map, where is

13 D in relation to A? ______

14 A in relation to C? ______

15 D in relation to B? ______

16 B in relation to D? ______

If A = 24, B = 12, C = 8, D = 4 and E = 2, give the answer to these calculations as a letter.

17 A ÷ B = ______

18 B + C + D = ______

19 (B – C) + D = ______

20 $\frac{DE}{E}$ = ______

Total

TEST 13: Mixed

Test time: 0 5 10 minutes

Find the three-letter word which can be added to the letters in capitals to make a new word. The new word will complete the sentence sensibly.

Example The cat sprang onto the MO. USE

1 The queen does not often wear a CN. ______

2 Nadia laid the table with four knives and KS. ______

3 That grocery S is more expensive than the one we use. ______

4 WE you knocked your head, you have a bruise. ______

5 The PR went out so we sat by candlelight all night. ______

Which one letter can be added to the front of all these words to make new words?

Example c are c at c rate c all

6	___ ass	___ ink	___ ray	___ at
7	___ how	___ at	___ even	___ and
8	___ our	___ oal	___ ox	___ ear
9	___ pen	___ range	___ at	___ men

Fill in the missing letters and numbers. The alphabet has been written out to help you.

A B C D E F G H I J K L M N O P Q R S T U V W X Y Z

Example AB is to CD as PQ is to RS.

10 GH is to KL as OP is to ____.

11 DF is to HJ as LN is to ____.

12 M8 is to L9 as K10 is to ____.

13 Mn is to Qr as Uv is to ____.

14 ZX is to VT as RP is to ____.

15 ST is to QR as OP is to ____.

Underline the word in the brackets closest in meaning to the word in capitals.

Example UNHAPPY (unkind death laughter sad friendly)

16	TRAIL	(measure	ward	pass	home	path)
17	HONOUR	(obey	lord	praise	order	hot)
18	PETROL	(oil	car	garage	engine	fuel)
19	DISCOVER	(hide	treasure	misplace	find	purchase)
20	CRIMSON	(blue	red	paint	flower	sky)

Total

TEST 14: Mixed

Test time: 0 5 10 minutes

Underline the two words, one from each group, which are closest in meaning.

Example (race, shop, start) (finish, begin, end)

1 (conceal, jelly, carnival) (show, mask, mould)

2 (danger, past, menace) (threaten, safety, annoy)

3 (orange, skin, huge) (body, colour, peel)

4 (tape, tune, melon) (melody, worm, violin)

5 (excited, happy, miserable) (smile, cry, sad)

Here are some symbol codes for four words. Match the right codes to the right words.

BOOT	BROW	TRAY	WARY
? Q + =	X 5 5 ?	£ + Q =	X Q 5 £

6 BOOT ____________

7 BROW ____________

8 TRAY ____________

9 WARY ____________

Using the same code, decode:

10 £ + Q ? ____________

11 Q 5 5 ? ____________

Give the missing numbers and letters in the following sequences.

Example	5	21	8	17	11	13	14	9
12	4	____	6	6	8	9	10	12
13	Q8	B5	Q10	B6	Q12	B7	____	B8
14	a17	a4	____	b5	c13	c6	d11	d7
15	42	F	35	H	____	J	21	L
16	3	5	6	____	9	9	12	11

If P = 2, Q = 3, R = 4, S = 14 and T = 15, find the answer to the following calculations.

17 $\frac{S}{P} + Q =$ ______

18 $S - QR =$ ______

19 $\frac{T}{Q} + R =$ ______

20 $S + PQ =$ ______

Total

Test 15: Mixed

Test time: 0 5 10 minutes

Add one letter to the word in capital letters to make a new word. The meaning of the new word is given in the clue.

Example PLAN simple plain

1 FEED released ________ 2 FIST before second ________

3 LENT sloped ________ 4 EAVES departs ________

Solve the problems by working out the letter codes. The alphabet has been written out to help you.

A B C D E F G H I J K L M N O P Q R S T U V W X Y Z

Example In a code, SECOND is written as UGEQPF.
How would you write THIRD? VJKTF

5 In a code, READY is written as SFBEZ. What is YARD? ________

6 In a code, BARKS is written as DCTMU. What is WIND? ________

7 In a code, TOKEN is written as RMICL. What is SOCK? ________

8 In a code, CRESS is written as BQDRR. What is BEST? ________

9 In a code, HOUSE is written as FMSQC. What is SHOE? ________

10 In a code, FARMS is written as HCTOU. What is FAIL? ________

Change the first word of the third pair in the same way as the other pairs to give a new word.

Example bind, hind bare, hare but, hut

11 bore, robe dome, mode file, ________

12 rail, bail rush, bush rook, ________

13 fare, fear lane, lean lake, ________

14 town, down tusk, dusk trip, ________

15 tale, late lose, sole newt, ________

16 doom, mood draw, ward flow, ________

If A = 15, B = 12, C = 8, D = 3 and E = 1, find the answer to the following calculations.

17 $A - C =$ ________

18 $(B + C) - E =$ ________

19 $\frac{A}{D} =$ ________

20 $(B - C) + D =$ ________

Total

Test 16: Mixed

Test time: 0 5 10 minutes

Underline the one word which cannot be made from the letters of the word in capital letters.

Example	STATIONERY	stone	tyres	ration	<u>nation</u>	noisy
1	GABERDINE	greed	engine	bread	drain	bride
2	DASTARDLY	tardy	yards	saddle	darts	astral
3	APOLOGISE	goals	spool	pages	igloo	police
4	NEWSPAPER	wasps	spear	prawns	spare	preen
5	APPARATUS	strap	sprat	parts	arrest	traps

Find the four-letter word hidden at the end of one word and the beginning of the next word. The order of the letters may not be changed.

Example The children had bat<u>s and</u> balls. sand

6 Mum buys fruit at the market. ____________

7 That is my best arrangement today. ____________

8 I will brush my teeth another time. ____________

9 Half the class wandered in late. ____________

10 Must I brush under the desks too? ____________

Move one letter from the first word and add it to the second word to make two new words.

Example	hunt	sip	hut	snip
11	play	sap	____________	____________
12	loft	lock	____________	____________
13	quite	have	____________	____________
14	stool	fits	____________	____________

Give the missing letters and numbers in the following sequences. The alphabet has been written out to help you.

A B C D E F G H I J K L M N O P Q R S T U V W X Y Z

Example	CQ	DP	EQ	FP	GQ	<u>HP</u>
15	CF	CG	DH	DI	____	EK
16	____	vE	wF	xG	yH	zI
17	DW	EV	FU	____	HS	IR
18	AB	____	CF	DH	EJ	FL
19	OP	RQ	ST	VU	WX	____
20	W13	Y11	____	Y7	W5	Y3

Time for a break! Go to Puzzle Page 43

Total

Test 17: Mixed

Test time: 0 5 10 minutes

Fill in the crosswords so that all the given words are included. You have been given one letter as a clue in each crossword.

1–3

SHARD STIFF

FIXED SNOWS

INDIA

	■	■	■	
	■	■	■	
F				

4–6

DARES ANGER

BRAIN BEARD

NOTES

	■		■	
	■		■	
	■		■	
		R		

Underline the two words which are the odd ones out in the following groups of words.

Example black <u>king</u> purple green <u>house</u>

7	hockey	cricket	ball	players	rounders
8	mouse	gerbil	rat	shark	cobra
9	oak	rose	sunflower	willow	tulip
10	book	television	newspaper	radio	magazine

Find the letter which will complete both pairs of words, ending the first word and starting the second. The same letter must be used for both pairs of words.

Example mea (t) able fi (t) ub

11 pin (___) ing tal (___) ey

12 sta (___) elp sill (___) es

13 pal (___) xam to (___) agle

14 gri (___) ie gras (___) ig

Here are some symbol codes for four words. Match the right code to the right word.

FADE	FIND	DEAN	NEED
! / @ %	@ £ £ %	! * % £	% £ * @

15 FADE ____________ **16** FIND ____________

17 DEAN ____________ **18** NEED ____________

Using the same code, decode:

19 % / @ £ ____________ **20** % £ * ! ____________

Total

TEST 18: Mixed

Test time: 0 5 10 minutes

Underline the one word in the brackets which will go equally well with both the pairs of words outside the brackets.

Example rush, attack cost, fee (price, hasten, strike, <u>charge</u>, money)

1	fete, festival	even, just	(party, level, proper, fair, equal)
2	foolhardy, reckless	spots, redness	(rush, rash, acne, fever, silly)
3	build, construct	force, cause	(order, make, stack, assemble, form)
4	difficult, tough	firm, inflexible	(easy, solid, hard, complicated, strong)
5	copy, mimic	shadow, trail	(follow, model, stalk, obey, lead)

The drama club is putting on a school play. Tessa and Harriet are going to make the costumes. Nadeen and Ben are going to build the sets. Francesca is going to help with the costumes but also do the lights. Mick is going to be the announcer for the first half of the play and Tessa will be the announcer for the second half. Mick will also be in charge of moving the props on and off the stage. Ben will help Mick when he is busy as the announcer.

6 Which two students are doing only one job? ____________ and ____________

7 Which student is helping with the costumes and the lights? ____________

8 How many students are helping make the costumes? ____________

9 Who will help move the props during the first half of the play? ____________

10 Which two students won't be busy during the play? ____________ and ____________

Find the letter which will end the first word and start the second word.

Example peac (h) ome

11 foo (___) humb **12** nex (___) rain **13** sta (___) elt **14** fee (___) ost

Rearrange the muddled letters in capitals to make a proper word. The answer will complete the sentence sensibly.

Example A BEZAR is an animal with stripes. ZEBRA

15 Under the stairs there is a dark BOADRPUC. ____________

16 The moon was shining so BRGTYIHL, it lit up the room. ____________

17 Vijay's father parked the car in the GGREAA. ____________

18 Sixteen, seventeen, IHENEEGT, nineteen. ____________

19 A young goose is called a LNGGISO. ____________

20 My mother enjoys doing crossword ZSZLEPU. ____________

Total

Test 19: Mixed

Test time: 0 5 10 minutes

Underline the two words in each line which are most similar in type or meaning.

Example dear pleasant poor extravagant expensive

1	steer	drive	garden	pond	swift
2	wed	flower	marry	church	feast
3	son	neighbour	daughter	friend	student
4	hair	heart	arm	neck	leg
5	school	scheme	letter	film	plan

Change the first word into the last word, by changing one letter at a time and making a new, different word in the middle.

Example CASE CASH LASH

6 CUBE ________ TUNE

7 PALM ________ CALF

8 PINE ________ PICK

9 WARM ________ YARN

Fill in the missing letters and numbers. The alphabet has been written out to help you.

A B C D E F G H I J K L M N O P Q R S T U V W X Y Z

Example AB is to CD as PQ is to RS.

10 JK is to LM as NO is to ____.

11 S16 is to T14 as U12 is to ____.

12 3FG is to 5GH as HI7 is to ____.

13 De is to Fg as Vw is to ____.

14 TR is to SQ as RP is to ____.

15 AD is to EH as IL is to ____.

Look at the first group of three words. The word in the middle has been made from the other two words. Complete the second group of three words in the same way, making a new word in the middle.

Example PAIN INTO TOOK ALSO SOON ONLY

16	PEEL	LOVE	OVEN	BOSS	________	HUTS
17	INTO	TORE	REAP	MOTH	________	INCH
18	SHUN	HUNT	WILT	SPAT	________	FISH
19	STAR	SOLD	HOLD	MOOR	________	LICE
20	KIND	KING	RUNG	ZERO	________	NEST

Total

Test 20: Mixed

Test time: 0 5 10 minutes

Underline the two words which are the odd ones out in the following groups of words.

Example black <u>king</u> purple green <u>house</u>

1	knife	fork	bowl	plate	spoon
2	stable	cow	elephant	sheep	sty
3	desk	ruler	class	rubber	pencil
4	spring	rain	winter	snow	summer
5	Australia	Wales	London	Sweden	Paris

Look at the first group of three words. The word in the middle has been made from the other two words. Complete the second group of three words in the same way, making a new word in the middle.

Example PA<u>IN</u> INTO <u>TO</u>OK ALSO SOON ONLY

6	PAST	STUN	UNTO	WIFE	______	ARCH
7	RAKE	RUST	MUST	STAR	______	BEAT
8	DRAG	DRIP	SNIP	FALL	______	SUNG
9	SPAR	PART	WENT	TREE	______	HOOF
10	SLUG	GONE	ONES	SLIM	______	AREA

Add one letter to the word in capital letters to make a new word. The meaning of the new word is given in the clue.

Example PLAN simple plain

11 RIGHT shiny ______ **12** BUSH broom ______

13 TONE rock ______ **14** FAME fire ______

15–20 **Here are two rows of houses in a street. Work out which families live in each house.**

22	24	26
	ARMADA AVENUE	
21	23	25

The Bennetts and the Ashtons live directly next door to each other on the even side of the street.
The Bennetts live in a lower number than the Ashtons.
The Fish family live directly opposite the Catt family.
The Bennetts live directly opposite to the Smiths who live in a higher number than the Catts, next door.
The Jones family are best friends with the Fish family.

Bennett ______ Ashton ______ Fish ______

Catt ______ Smith ______ Jones ______

Total

Test 21: Mixed

Test time: 0 5 10 minutes

Give the missing numbers and letters in the following sequences.

Example	2	4	6	8	10	12
1	14	24	___	44	54	64
2	3	___	11	15	19	23
3	___	10	15	20	25	30
4	4	5	7	10	___	19
5	X13	Y11	Z9	___	Y5	Z3
6	64	32	16	8	4	___

Solve the problems by working out the codes.

7 If the code for x o – + is DOWN, what does the code + o x stand for? ________

8 If the code for < > / \ is SANG, what does the code \ > < stand for? ________

9 If the code for APPQ is DOOR, what does the code QPA stand for? ________

10 If the code for = – ~ \ is THIS, what does the code \ ~ = stand for? ________

Rearrange the letters in capitals to make another word. The new word has something to do with the first two words.

Example	spot	soil	SAINT	STAIN
11	loved	adored	READ	________
12	light	fire	PARKS	________
13	painful	hurting	ROSE	________
14	killed	dead	NAILS	________
15	frozen	water	DICE	________
16	ruler	guide	DEALER	________

Find a word that can be put in front of each of the following words to make new compound words.

Example	cast	fall	ward	pour	down
17	side	vent	to	sure	________
18	knob	mat	step	bell	________
19	times	where	thing	one	________
20	world	wear	water	stand	________

Total

TEST 22: Mixed

Test time: 0 5 10 minutes

Find the three-letter word which can be added to the letters in capitals to make a new word. The new word will complete the sentence sensibly.

Example The cat sprang onto the MO. USE

1 I hope we win some G medals at the Olympics. ______
2 My grandmother wears a HING aid. ______
3 Have a bowl of STBERRIES and cream. ______
4 Would you like jam and TER on your bread? ______
5 During the lunch H Tom plays football. ______

Underline the one word which can be made from the letters of the word in capital letters.

Example CHAMPION camping notch peach cramp <u>chimp</u>

6	KINDEST	stink	desks	token	taste	kings
7	ELEPHANT	thank	neater	paler	panel	heaps
8	PARTITION	nation	print	parting	north	trains
9	CONTAINER	energy	conker	narrow	counter	ration
10	BRIGHTLY	height	truly	light	tight	highly

Remove one letter from the word in capital letters to leave a new word. The meaning of the new word is given in the clue.

Example AUNT an insect ANT

11 DRIVE plunge ______
12 GRIND smile ______
13 BLAST final ______
14 TRANCE copy ______

Give the missing letters and numbers in the following sequences. The alphabet has been written out to help you.

A B C D E F G H I J K L M N O P Q R S T U V W X Y Z

Example CQ DP EQ FP GQ <u>HP</u>

15	Z12	Y10	X8	W6	V4	____
16	____	GW	HV	IU	JT	KS
17	MZ	MY	____	NW	OV	OU
18	kV	lU	mT	____	oR	pQ
19	Ny	____	Pw	Qv	Ru	St
20	AB	DC	EF	HG	____	LK

Total

Test 23: Mixed

Test time: 0 5 10 minutes

Underline two words, one from each group, that go together to form a new word. The word in the first group always comes first.

Example (hand, <u>green</u>, for) (light, <u>house</u>, sure)

1	(hand, foot, close)	(sore, writing, reading)
2	(dripping, wet, towel)	(suit, clothes, tea)
3	(price, much, too)	(more, kind, less)
4	(car, engine, wheel)	(boot, near, barrow)

Give the missing numbers and letters in the following sequences.

Example 5 21 8 17 11 13 <u>14</u> 9

5	3	10	5	11	7	12	___	13
6	___	r	9	s	12	t	15	u
7	R15	R1	___	S2	T17	T3	U18	U4
8	A7	1a	B7	2b	C7	3c	D7	___
9	1	2	3	5	5	___	7	11

Underline the pair of words most similar in meaning.

Example come, go <u>roam, wander</u> ear, fare

10	whisper, shout	discuss, talk	argue, agree
11	block, lump	chunk, morsel	part, whole
12	up, down	outside, exterior	under, on
13	high, low	loud, faint	quiet, hushed
14	find, keep	enter, exit	fall, tumble

Change the first word of the third pair in the same way as the other pairs to give a new word.

Example bind, hind bare, hare but, <u>hut</u>

15	wane, wean	pale, peal	bare, ___________
16	top, lop	tight, light	tax, ___________
17	pals, slap	deer, reed	draw, ___________
18	made, dame	file, life	lope, ___________
19	mean, mane	weak, wake	team, ___________
20	chin, thin	chat, that	chose, ___________

Total

Answers

Test 1: Similars and Opposites

1 rigid, stiff
2 basin, bath
3 apple, pear
4 clear, obvious
5 boat, yacht
6 tidy, messy
7 soft, hard
8 solid, liquid
9 confident, shy
10 over, under
11 complete, whole
12 grip, clasp
13 problem, difficulty
14 appear, arrive
15 feel, touch
16 take
17 bumpy
18 above
19 dull
20 beginning

Test 2: Sorting Words 1

1 part
2 hit
3 trunk
4 bright
5 plant
6 socks, shoes
7 bicycle, skateboard
8 hat, glove
9 middle, bottom
10 sausage, sick
11 CONTINENTS
12 ELECTRIC
13 FRONT
14 SEASIDE
15 CHOCOLATE
16 dairy, cows
17 other, twenty
18 some, you
19 door, the
20 red, shirt

Test 3: Sorting Words 2

1 CHAIR
2 SPEND
3 PROOF
4 SHALLOW
5 WHEEL
6 shoe
7 lord
8 tell
9 stale
10 break
11 LANCE CLEAN
12 SLOPE POLES
13 FLAIR FRAIL
14 WINGS SWING
15 LEAST TALES
16 SEAT
17 LEAP
18 ROPE
19 DROP
20 TEACH

Test 4: Selecting Words

1 footpath
2 woodland
3 strawberry
4 handyman
5 whitewash
6 y
7 k
8 e
9 r
10 w
11 oars rowed shore
12 rocket sky station
13 drove into turned
14 uncle mother's brother
15 down fragrant garden
16 month
17 bluff
18 argue
19 quince
20 brisk

Test 5: Finding Words

1 form
2 hiss
3 hand
4 tore
5 belt
6 AIR
7 DAY
8 HUT
9 SHE
10 OWL
11 black
12 hand
13 tea
14 up
15 life
16 fir away
17 arch comb
18 ever yearly
19 each fleet
20 limb patch

Test 6: Alphabetical Order and Substitution

1 floor
2 hilly
3 adept
4 begins
5 deity
6 little
7 galaxy
8 fairness
9 chariot
10 tears
11 12
12 60
13 8
14 15
15 11
16 C
17 E
18 B
19 A
20 D

Test 7: Word Progressions

1 TREE
2 STAR
3 EAST
4 CLAM
5 EXIT
6 BIND
7 TALK
8 BELL
9 SING
10 FARE
11 seal
12 felt
13 rail
14 fall
15 peek
16 16
17 2
18 15
19 8
20 20

Test 8: Logic

1–2 Tiles are a type of roof covering.
A house needs a roof.
3–4 Helmets may be part of a police officer's uniform.
Police officers help to catch people who break the law.
5–9 1 floppy eared
2 brown and white
3 white
4 black
5 fat
10 Mike
11 5
12 Tom
13 1
14 Sam
15–20 novels D
reference books F
CDs C
school books E
photographs A
DVDs B

Test 9: Codes

1 6538
2 6138
3 6440
4 0138
5 DONE
6 FOR
7 CAME
8 ROPE
9 RAT
10 MET
11 CJUT
12 OCUV
13 CFFO
14 GDDK
15 DMSJ
16 MADE
17 NEED
18 GERM
19 DEEP
20 BITE

Test 10: Sequences

1 vein, blood
2 summer, hot
3 gills, lungs
4 start, finish
5 break, stop
6 WU
7 Pt
8 YZ
9 M9
10 NP
11 4
12 12
13 9
14 303
15 23v
16 IM
17 NP
18 QS
19 QP
20 Ht

Test 11: Mixed

1 RUBBER
2 BUCKET
3 JANUARY
4 STING
5 EXPLOSION
6 CHRISTMAS
7 ACEILPS
8 L
9 ACEHPR
10 H
11 stain
12 fear
13 store
14 save
15 vile
16 NPQR
17 FERNN
18 342
19 zyb
20 YTRX

Test 12: Mixed

1 brooch
2 chimney
3 penny
4 danger
5 SEAT
6 DOG
7 TIME
8 BAR
9 horse
10 bed
11 two
12 floor
13 west
14 north-east
15 north-west
16 south-east
17 E
18 A
19 C
20 D

Test 13: Mixed

1 ROW
2 FOR
3 HOP
4 HER
5 OWE
6 p
7 s
8 f
9 o
10 ST
11 PR
12 J11
13 Yz
14 NL
15 MN
16 path
17 praise
18 fuel
19 find
20 red

Test 14: Mixed

1 conceal, mask
2 menace, threaten
3 skin, peel
4 tune, melody
5 miserable, sad
6 X 5 5 ?
7 X Q 5 £
8 ? Q + =
9 £ + Q =
10 WART
11 ROOT
12 3
13 Q14
14 b15
15 28
16 7
17 10
18 2
19 9
20 20

Test 15: Mixed

1 FREED
2 FIRST
3 LEANT
4 LEAVES
5 ZBSE
6 YKPF
7 QMAI
8 ADRS
9 QFMC
10 HCKN
11 life
12 book
13 leak
14 drip
15 went
16 wolf
17 7
18 19
19 5
20 7

Test 16: Mixed

1 engine
2 saddle
3 police
4 wasps
5 arrest
6 them
7 star
8 than
9 swan
10 shun
11 pay, slap
12 lot, flock
13 quit, heave
14 tool, fists
15 EJ
16 uD
17 GT
18 BD
19 ZY
20 W9

Test 17: Mixed

1–3

S	N	O	W	S
T				H
I	N	D	I	A
F				R
F	I	X	E	D

4–6

B	R	A	I	N
E		N		O
A		G		T
R		E		E
D	A	R	E	S

7 ball, players
8 shark, cobra
9 oak, willow
10 television, radio
11 k
12 y
13 e
14 p
15 ! * % £
16 ! / @ %
17 % £ * @
18 @ £ £ %
19 DINE
20 DEAF

Test 18: Mixed

1 fair
2 rash
3 make
4 hard
5 follow
6 Harriet and Nadeen
7 Francesca
8 3
9 Ben
10 Harriet and Nadeen
11 t
12 t
13 b
14 l
15 CUPBOARD
16 BRIGHTLY
17 GARAGE
18 EIGHTEEN
19 GOSLING
20 PUZZLES

Test 19: Mixed

1 steer, drive
2 wed, marry
3 son, daughter
4 arm, leg
5 scheme, plan
6 TUBE
7 CALM
8 PINK
9 WARN
10 PQ
11 V10
12 IJ9
13 Xy
14 QO
15 MP
16 SHUT
17 THIN
18 PATH
19 MICE
20 ZEST

Test 20: Mixed

1 bowl, plate
2 stable, sty
3 desk, class
4 rain, snow
5 London, Paris
6 FEAR
7 SEAT
8 FANG
9 REEF
10 MARE
11 BRIGHT
12 BRUSH
13 STONE
14 FLAME
15 24
16 26
17 22
18 21
19 23
20 25

Test 21: Mixed

1 34
2 7
3 5
4 14
5 X7
6 2
7 NOD
8 GAS
9 ROD
10 SIT
11 DEAR
12 SPARK
13 SORE
14 SLAIN
15 ICED
16 LEADER
17 in
18 door
19 some
20 under

Test 22: Mixed

1 OLD
2 EAR
3 RAW
4 BUT
5 OUR
6 stink
7 panel
8 print
9 ration
10 light
11 DIVE
12 GRIN
13 LAST
14 TRACE
15 U2
16 FX
17 NX
18 nS
19 Ox
20 IJ

Test 23: Mixed

1 handwriting
2 wetsuit
3 priceless
4 wheelbarrow
5 9
6 6
7 S16
8 4d
9 8
10 discuss, talk
11 block, lump
12 outside, exterior
13 quiet, hushed
14 fall, tumble
15 bear
16 lax
17 ward
18 pole
19 tame
20 those

Test 24: Mixed

1 8F9
2 13
3 17
4 15H
5 love
6 item
7 sour
8 thin
9 them
10 shoot, fire
11 train, teach
12 pair, two
13 diary, journal
14 road, street
15 MBOE
16 LHMS

17 PCKN
18 CDRJ
19 CBMM
20 EPGB

Test 25: Mixed

1 kind, cruel
2 more, less
3 clean, dirty
4 answer, question
5 begin, turn
6 at, were
7 channels, television
8 hose, garden
9 burnt, spread
10 swing, sister
11 25
12 15e
13 20
14 9
15 A3
16 PARTS STRAP
17 LEAPT PLATE
18 SPOOL LOOPS
19 DEALER LEADER
20 STEAL LEAST

Test 26: Mixed

1 PLAY
2 EATS
3 FOOL
4 ONCE
5 SNOW
6 fast
7 straight-forward
8 correct
9 frequent
10 mature
11 t
12 h
13 s
14 l
15 EG
16 JI
17 RS
18 NL
19 9TU
20 W55

Test 27: Mixed

1 relaxed, strict
2 soft, firm
3 wealthy, poor
4 stale, fresh
5 elephants, river, trunks
6 road, right, traffic
7 ran, ball, goal
8 playground, put on, coats
9 pencil, over, bin
10 exciting, book, chapter
11 5
12 6
13 1
14 40
15 WEED
16 FIRM
17 HURT
18 FOUR
19 LIFE
20 BIRD

Test 28: Mixed

1 PEACH CHEAP
2 TOAST STOAT
3 TRACE CRATE
4 ASLEEP PLEASE
5 STATE TASTE
6 beef, cow
7 radio, listen
8 black, grey
9 dawn, dusk
10 apple, fruit
11 bedroom, sleep
12 Ann
13 Beth
14 Chloe
15 3
16 LOMN
17 TRA
18 SBYF
19 AZC
20 WZTL

Test 29: Mixed

1 b
2 l
3 s
4 h
5 first
6 accent
7 blot
8 hilly
9 JADE
10 ICED
11 6145
12 8554
13–14 Cars travel on roads. Roads are for vehicles to travel on.
15–16 My cat is related to a lion. The cat family includes tigers.
17 6
18 11
19 22
20 12

Test 30: Mixed

1 is, at
2 road, bus
3 for, had
4 go, please
5 trees, leaves
6 in, put
7 wholesome
8 upset
9 indeed
10 windscreen
11 1836
12 6481
13 3814
14 1446
15 SEAT
16 dearest
17 beast
18 please
19 yearn
20 eager

Test 31: Mixed

1–3

P	L	A	N	K
	E		O	
W	A	R	T	S
	V		E	
S	E	N	D	S

4–6

B	R	A	N	D
A				R
R	A	N	G	E
B				A
S	H	R	E	D

7 905
8 @ $! %
9 UQB
10 × − = +
11 marmalade
12 tiger
13 collar
14 C B
15 D B
16 A D
17 whole, part
18 delicate, hardy
19 believe, doubt
20 anxious, carefree

Test 32: Mixed

1 LEAP
2 LEMON
3 QUIET
4 SLEET
5 DIAL
6 CHARM
7 post
8 sun
9 child
10 foot
11 N
12 M
13 N
14 L
15 6
16 424
17 12
18 D42
19 3
20 17

Test 33: Mixed

1 PJ
2 IR
3 E5
4 DP
5 GH
6 SB
7 b
8 a
9 g
10 t
11 harm
12 iced
13 then
14 team
15 leaf
16 stench, smell
17 join, connect
18 bend, curve
19 pen, pencil
20 need, require

Test 34: Mixed

1 WENT
2 DRAB
3 FAME
4 EACH
5 FLAT
6 bedrooms
7 ink
8 a nose
9 long ears
10–15 card F
plastics G
brown glass B
shoes E
green glass C
newspapers A
16 sketch
17 fowl
18 quick
19 light
20 rule

Test 35: Mixed

1–3

P	I	T	C	H
A		O		O
T		K		N
H		E		E
S	U	N	N	Y

4–6

P	A	R	C	H
O		O		O
K	I	T	E	S
E		O		T
R		R		S

7 present
8 jam
9 quick
10 well
11 LIMB
12 BUY
13 PEAR
14 PARK
15 NM
16 Gt
17 1SQ
18 RT
19 S5
20 IG

Test 36: Mixed

1 S11
2 14
3 9
4 40
5 X9
6 8
7 1
8 10
9 2
10 CRAB
11 WILL
12 POLE
13 POST
14 LOOP
15 FILE
16 alive
17 expensive
18 release
19 sluggish
20 patterned

Test 37: Mixed

1 5793
2 1379
3 9375
4 1375
5 BREAD
6 hooves, paws
7 cricket, hockey
8 difficult, easy
9 loose, tight
10 hurl, toss
11 entrance, arrival
12–15 *Give one mark for each two correct answers:* Spain A, shirt C, yellow B, orange B, hat C, van D, Norway A, bus D
16 mend
17 tender
18 value
19 hollow
20 ignorant

Test 38: Mixed

1 higher
2 stork
3 paths
4 front
5 torch
6 mauls
7 skate
8 throne
9 braid
10 snare
11 fan, seal
12 ear, brainy
13 sore, bend
14 heat, thorn
15 GN
16 Z11
17 Gr
18 JK
19 VI
20 SL

Test 39: Mixed

1 bizarre, weird
2 prize, value
3 near, by
4 precious, valuable
5 tatters, shreds
6 DATE
7 BOAT
8 CART
9 PAIN
10 E
11 B
12 B
13 E
14–15 The Atlantic is one of the world's oceans.
There are oceans in the world.
16 WIG
17 WIT
18 KEEP
19 ATOM
20 LOT

Test 40: Mixed

1 HIDE
2 FEED
3 4935
4 31754
5 4516
6 <u>plate</u>, knife
7 <u>thunder</u>, lightning
8 <u>seagulls</u>, sheep
9 <u>newsagent</u>, newspapers
10 <u>car</u>, man
11 <u>red</u>, green
12 15
13 collie
14 10
15 dalmatian
16 pet, baby
17 slow, kind
18 remove, carry
19 frame, crayon
20 rude, scowling

Puzzle 1

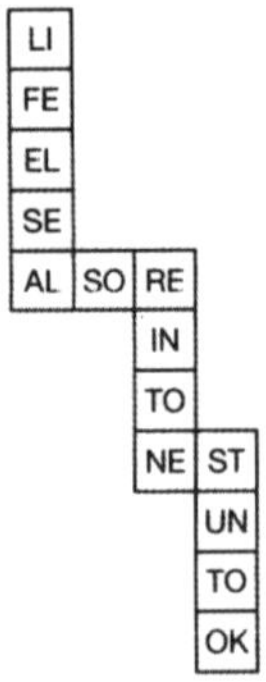

Puzzle 2

CAMP
ROUND **FIRE**
WATER **WORK** PLACE
WHEEL SHOP **OUT** MAT
CHAIR FRONT SIDE **DOOR** TIN
TABLE WAYS **MAN** STOP
CLOTH **AGE** KIND
LESS HEARTED
ON

TURN
OVER NIP
HAND GROWN PER
SOME FULL UP FORM
HOW TIME LOAD ALL LESS
EVER SHARE RIGHT ROUND
GREEN HOLDER WING
HOUSE MIRROR
WIFE

Puzzle 3

ROUTE C

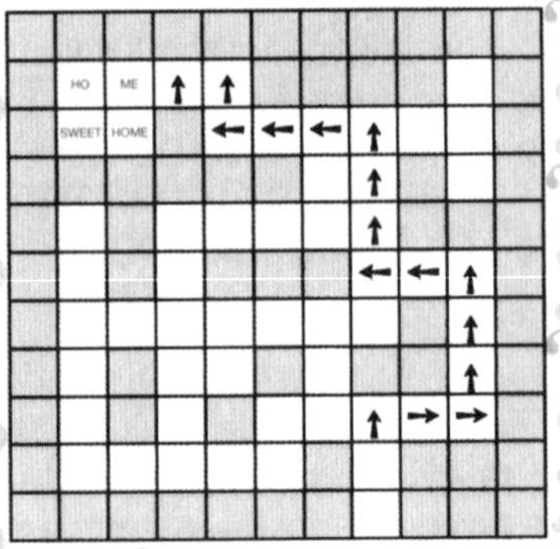

Puzzle 4

Any 5 words that can be made from each of the listed words, for example:

FLOWER
row wore lower
for owe wolf owl

GARDEN
den dare anger
red darn range

SPRING
pig grin sprig
rig ring grins pin

LEAVES
veal leave ale
seal slave see

Puzzle 5

Children	Colour of Dice	Number of Sixes
Mia	red	12
Nathan	yellow	7
Rohan	blue	14
Sita	green	5

Test 24: Mixed

Test time: 0 5 10 minutes

Give the missing numbers and letters in the following sequences.

Example	2	4	6	8	10	12
1	3A4	4B5	5C6	6D7	7E8	____
2	9	____	17	21	25	29
3	13	15	____	19	21	23
4	____	20H	25G	30G	35F	40F

Find the four-letter word hidden at the end of one word and the beginning of the next word. The order of the letters may not be changed.

Example The children had bats and balls. sand

5 The policeman's helmet fell over his eyes. ____________

6 She gave me my favourite magazine. ____________

7 We will miss our turn. ____________

8 The twins are both in the show. ____________

9 "Best foot forwards!" shouted the major. ____________

Underline the two words, one from each group, which are closest in meaning.

Example	(race, shop, start)	(finish, begin, end)
10	(wood, camp, shoot)	(tent, metal, fire)
11	(bus, train, chair)	(school, sit, teach)
12	(pair, many, plenty)	(single, two, none)
13	(note, diary, poem)	(drawing, map, journal)
14	(path, road, pavement)	(park, street, city)

Solve the problems by working out the letter codes. The alphabet has been written out to help you.

A B C D E F G H I J K L M N O P Q R S T U V W X Y Z

Example In a code, SECOND is written as UGEQPF. How would you write THIRD? VJKTF

15 In a code, LAYER is written as MBZFS. What is LAND? ____________

16 In a code, SLEEP is written as RKDDO. What is MINT? ____________

17 In a code, PLAIN is written as RNCKP. What is NAIL? ____________

18 In a code, GUESS is written as FTDRR. What is DESK? ____________

19 In a code, THROW is written as UISPX. What is BALL? ____________

20 In a code, FUDGE is written as DSBEC. What is GRID? ____________

Time for a break! Go to Puzzle Page 44

Total

Test 25: Mixed

Test time: 0 5 10 minutes

Underline the two words, one from each group, which are most opposite in meaning.

Example (dawn, early, wake) (late, stop, sunrise)

1 (nurse, divide, kind) (sort, cruel, caring)

2 (most, more, least) (less, lose, some)

3 (clean, misty, clear) (dirty, spotless, shiny)

4 (speak, talk, answer) (question, reply, whisper)

Find and underline the two words which need to change places for the sentence to make sense.

Example She went to letter the write.

5 Begin over your papers and turn.

6 There at over thirty children were the party.

7 The channels will not change television.

8 He watered the hose with a garden.

9 Edith burnt butter on her spread toast.

10 Sometimes I push my little swing on the sister.

Give the missing numbers and letters in the following sequences.

Example	5	21	8	17	11	13	14	9
11	6	30	7	____	8	20	9	15
12	11e	20y	13e	15y	____	10y	17e	5y
13	C	14	E	17	G	____	I	23
14	10	12	8	____	6	6	4	3
15	A9	X5	A7	X5	A5	X5	____	X5

Underline the two words which are made from the same letters.

Example	TAP	PET	TEA	POT	EAT
16	PARTS	STARE	STRAP	RESTS	PRESS
17	STEEL	LEAST	TAUPE	LEAPT	PLATE
18	PROUD	SPOOL	LOOPS	DROOP	SOUPS
19	DEALER	READER	TREADS	LEADER	SPREAD
20	STEAL	LEAST	STOOL	LASTS	STALL

Total

TEST 26: Mixed

Test time: 0 5 10 minutes

Look at the first group of three words. The word in the middle has been made from the other two words. Complete the second group of three words in the same way, making a new word in the middle.

Example	PAIN	INTO	TOOK	ALSO	SOON	ONLY
1	KIND	DROP	ROPE	DEEP	______	LAYS
2	DRAG	RAGE	FINE	NEAT	______	CATS
3	WANT	WIRE	FIRE	FOOT	______	TOOL
4	LATE	TEST	STOW	MOON	______	CENT
5	PINE	PEAT	WHAT	STUN	______	FLOW

Underline one word in the brackets which is most opposite in meaning to the word in capitals.

Example	WIDE	(broad	vague	long	narrow	motorway)
6	SLOW	(loose	fast	last	sluggish	late)
7	TRICKY	(awkward	clever	difficult	straightforward	sly)
8	WRONG	(correct	faulty	mistaken	untrue	unsure)
9	RARE	(unusual	front	back	smooth	frequent)
10	IMMATURE	(unripe	childish	young	mature	long)

Which one letter can be added to the front of all these words to make new words?

Example c are c at c rate c all

11 ___ each ___ ouch ___ ear ___ high

12 ___ our ___ ill ___ earth ___ air

13 ___ mile ___ tuck ___ pill ___ pin

14 ___ ice ___ edge ___ earn ___ ate

Fill in the missing letters and numbers. The alphabet has been written out to help you.

A B C D E F G H I J K L M N O P Q R S T U V W X Y Z

Example AB is to CD as PQ is to RS.

15 BD is to CE as DF is to ___.

16 PO is to NM as LK is to ___.

17 Lm is to No as Pq is to ___.

18 QO is to PN as OM is to ___.

19 15QR is to 13RS as 11ST is to ___.

20 T22 is to U33 as V44 is to ___.

Total

TEST 27: Mixed

Test time: 0 5 10 minutes

Underline the pair of words most opposite in meaning.

Example cup, mug coffee, milk <u>hot, cold</u>

1	relaxed, strict	stone, rock	garden, house
2	pillow, bed	cushion, chair	soft, firm
3	luxury, riches	wealthy, poor	money, coins
4	stale, fresh	calm, peaceful	magical, fantastic

Complete the following sentences by selecting the most sensible word from each group of words given in the brackets. Underline the words selected.

Example The (<u>children,</u> books, foxes) carried the (houses, <u>books,</u> steps) home from the (greengrocer, <u>library</u>, factory).

5 As the (elephants, lions, bears) waded across the (high street, river, mountain) they held their (passengers, trunks, suitcases) up high to keep them out of the water.

6 At four o'clock we cross the (lake, road, shop) outside school, looking left and (behind, wrong, right) because of the busy (traffic, police car, day).

7 John quickly (ran, tripped, crept) up the pitch dribbling the (bib, ball, secret) and scored the first (goal, test, baby) of the match.

8 As it is cold outside in the (fridge, playground, classroom), please (put on, take off, eat) your (shoes, coats, apples).

9 Clare, please sharpen your (pen, book, pencil) (over, under, beside) the (bed, mouse, bin).

10 I am already halfway through my very (exciting, eager, delicate) new (pillow, label, book) in the sixth (word, chapter, line).

If V = 10, W = 4, X = 3, Y = 1 and Z = 2, find the answer to the following calculations.

11 $\frac{V}{Z}$ = ______ 12 (YZ) + W = ______ 13 (XY) − Z = ______ 14 VW = ______

Solve the problems by working out the letter codes. The alphabet has been written out to help you.

A B C D E F G H I J K L M N O P Q R S T U V W X Y Z

Example In a code, SECOND is written as UGEQPF. Decode VJKTF. THIRD

15 In a code, WEDGE is written as UCBEC. Decode UCCB. ______

16 In a code, STERN is written as RSDQM. Decode EHQL. ______

17 In a code, HARSH is written as JCTUJ. Decode JWTV. ______

18 In a code, BIRCH is written as CJSDI. Decode GPVS. ______

19 In a code, RIFLE is written as QHEKD. Decode KHED. ______

20 In a code, BADGE is written as CBEHF. Decode CJSE. ______

Total

Test 28: Mixed

Test time: 0 5 10 minutes

Underline the two words which are made from the same letters.

Example	TAP	PET	<u>TEA</u>	POT	<u>EAT</u>
1	PERCH	CHURCH	PEACH	CHIRP	CHEAP
2	TOAST	STOAT	START	TASTE	ROAST
3	CARTS	SHARK	TRACE	STARK	CRATE
4	PRAISE	ASLEEP	STRIPE	PLEASE	SPITE
5	STRAW	WASPS	STATE	SPATE	TASTE

Choose two words, one from each set of brackets, to complete the sentence in the best way.

Example Smile is to happiness as (drink, <u>tear</u>, shout) is to (whisper, laugh, <u>sorrow</u>).

6 Pork is to pig as (chops, beef, fish) is to (sheep, cow, chicken).

7 Television is to watch as (radio, ladder, chair) is to (talk, sound, listen).

8 Red is to pink as (black, colour, paint) is to (dark, grey, white).

9 Sunrise is to sunset as (cloudy, afternoon, dawn) is to (dusk, morning, breakfast).

10 Carrot is to vegetable as (cabbage, apple, lettuce) is to (pear, potato, fruit).

11 Kitchen is to cook as (bathroom, bedroom, playroom) is to (sleep, eat, drive).

Some girls were asked which books they had with them in their bags one afternoon.
Ann, Mira and Chloe had spelling books.
Davina and Ann had library books.
Beth had a photo album.
Mira and Chloe had Maths books.
They all had reading books except for Mira.

12 Who had a spelling book as well as a library book? ____________

13 Who did not have a Maths or a library book? ____________

14 Who had a reading book and a Maths book? ____________

15 How many books did Ann have? ____________

Solve the problems by working out the codes.

16 If the code for CATCH is LMNLO, what is the code for CHAT? ____________

17 If the code for BOOKS is ARRNT, what is the code for SOB? ____________

18 If the code for ACTOR is FBYBS, what is the code for ROTA? ____________

19 If the code for TRAIN is CZALP, what is the code for ART? ____________

20 If the code for PATCH is WZLTO, what is the code for PACT? ____________

Total

TEST 29: Mixed

Test time: 0 5 10 minutes

Find the letter which will end the first word and start the second word.

Example peac (h) ome

1 cra (___) oxes **2** gir (___) ast **3** dog (___) oup **4** bat (___) arp

Underline the word in each line that has its letters in alphabetical order.

5	fast	force	fixes	first	fusion
6	abacus	alert	accent	actual	agent
7	blood	blot	blame	blown	bloom
8	hinge	height	hippo	humus	hilly

If the letters of the alphabet are coded as A = 1, B = 2, C = 3 and so on, what words would these codes make?

9	10	1	4	5	________
10	9	3	5	4	________

Encode these words using the same code as above.

11 FADE ________ **12** HEED ________

Read the statements and then underline two of the five options below. that must be true given the information.

13–14 'Cars and vans are vehicles. All vehicles travel on the road.'

Only vans travel on the road.
Cars travel on roads.
All vehicles are cars.
Vans drive fast.
Roads are for vehicles to travel on.

15–16 'Lions and tigers are related. They are all members of the cat family.'

My cat is a lion.
My cat is related to a lion.
All cats are tigers.
The cat family includes tigers.
Lions eat tigers.

Give the missing numbers in the following sequences.

Example 2 4 6 8 10 12

17	3	4	___	9	13	18
18	7	___	15	19	23	27
19	16	18	20	___	24	26
20	20	18	16	14	___	10

Total

TEST 30: Mixed

Test time: 0 5 10 minutes

Find and underline the two words which need to change places for the sentence to make sense.

Example She went to letter the write.

1 Is the bottom of the garden there at a shed.
2 The road stopped at the bottom of the bus.
3 Jake for eggs and bacon had breakfast.
4 Go please to bed now.
5 The trees fell off the leaves.
6 She in her fork and knife put the dishwasher.

Underline two words, one from each group, that go together to form a new word. The word in the first group always comes first.

Example (hand, green, for) (light, house, sure)

7 (quarter, whole, half) (turn, size, some)
8 (bent, side, up) (cash, fall, set)
9 (for, in, by) (spot, deed, date)
10 (wind, black, screw) (wood, screen, barn)

Here are the number codes for four words. Match the right code to the right word.

MAST	SAME	TEAM	MEET
1446	1836	3814	6481

11 MAST ____________ 12 TEAM ____________
13 SAME ____________ 14 MEET ____________

Using the same code, decode:

15 3486 ____________

Underline the one word which cannot be made from the letters of the word in capital letters.

Example STATIONERY stone tyres ration nation noisy

16	BROADEST	strode	trade	breast	toads	dearest
17	BECAUSE	sauce	beast	cease	case	cubes
18	PLANETS	stale	plant	steal	please	staple
19	BEARING	yearn	grain	brine	bring	brain
20	STRANGER	grate	range	stare	great	eager

Total

Test 31: Mixed

Test time: 0 5 10 minutes

Fill in the crosswords so that all the given words are included. You have been given one letter as a clue in each crossword.

1–3

NOTED PLANK
SENDS WARTS
LEAVE

■		■		■
■		■		■
	E			

4–6

BRAND BARBS
DREAD SHRED
RANGE

	■	■	■	
			G	
	■	■	■	

Solve the problems by working out the codes.

7 If 8059 stands for MEND, what is DEN? ____________

8 If % ! $ @ stands for PART, what is TRAP? ____________

9 If BZQU stands for PLAY, what is YAP? ____________

10 If + − = × stands for DOLT, what is TOLD? ____________

Underline the word in the brackets which goes best with the words given outside the brackets.

Example word, paragraph, sentence (pen, cap, <u>letter</u>, top, stop)

11 cereal, toast, milk (curry, marmalade, gravy, wine, beetroot)

12 tail, stripes, fangs (zebra, wolf, tiger, snail, hippo)

13 sleeve, buttonhole, pocket (jeans, cloth, scarf, collar, fashion)

Look at these groups of words.

A	B	C	D
elephant	wardrobe	shark	melon
cat	chair	cod	apple
sheep	bed	salmon	peach

Choose the correct group for each of the words below. Write in the letter.

14–16 dogfish ____ cupboard ____ banana ____ table ____ fox ____ grapes ____

Underline the two words, one from each group, which are the most opposite in meaning.

Example (dawn, <u>early</u>, wake) (<u>late</u>, stop, sunrise)

17 (spare, whole, eager) (complete, part, quick)

18 (apart, instant, delicate) (hardy, course, dainty)

19 (believe, touch, pull) (find, take, doubt)

20 (open, anxious, free) (carefree, concerned, careful)

Total

Test 32: Mixed

Test time: 0 5 10 minutes

Rearrange the letters in capitals to make another word. The new word has something to do with the first two words or phrases.

Example	spot	soil	SAINT	STAIN
1	jump	hop	PEAL	______
2	fruit	citrus	MELON	______
3	silent	peaceful	QUITE	______
4	snowy	icy rain	STEEL	______
5	disk	clock face	LAID	______
6	enchant	dazzle	MARCH	______

Find a word that can be put in front of each of the following words to make new, compound words.

Example	cast	fall	ward	pour	down
7	card	box	code	man	______
8	burn	glasses	set	shine	______
9	hood	proof	like	minder	______
10	print	path	bridge	ball	______

If J = 1, K = 2, L = 3, M = 6 and N = 12, find the answer to the following. Write your answer as a letter.

11 $J + K + L + M =$ ____ **12** $\frac{N}{K} =$ ____

13 $MK =$ ____ **14** $M - L =$ ____

Give the missing numbers and letters in the following sequences.

Example	2	4	6	8	10	12
15	3	1	____	1	9	1
16	121	222	323	____	525	626
17	18	15	____	9	6	3
18	____	E35	F28	D21	E14	F7
19	96	48	24	12	6	____
20	7	8	10	13	____	22

Time for a break! Go to Puzzle Page 45

Total

Test 33: Mixed

Test time: 0 5 10 minutes

Give the missing letters and numbers in the following sequences. The alphabet has been written out to help you.

A B C D E F G H I J K L M N O P Q R S T U V W X Y Z

Example	CQ	DP	EQ	FP	GQ	HP
1	TH	SH	RI	QI	____	OJ
2	jT	kS	____	mQ	nP	oO
3	E8	F7	G6	____	F4	G3
4	BO	____	FQ	HR	JS	LT
5	____	HJ	IL	JN	KP	LR
6	SF	ME	SD	MC	____	MA

Find the letter which will complete both pairs of words, ending the first word and starting the second. The same letter must be used for both sets of words.

Example mea (t) able fi (t) ub

7 cri (___) ook sta (___) usy
8 are (___) pple gal (___) sk
9 dra (___) one win (___) lory
10 ca (___) oken goa (___) ail

Find the four-letter word hidden at the end of one word and the beginning of the next word. The order of the letters may not be changed.

Example The children had bat<u>s and</u> balls. sand

11 Both armies were exhausted. ________
12 Mary thinks orange juice drinks are best. ________
13 Pass the netball to Natasha. ________
14 The head teacher looked quite amused. ________
15 The bread was stale after a few days. ________

Underline the two words in each line which are most similar in type or meaning.

Example	<u>dear</u>	pleasant	poor	extravagant	<u>expensive</u>
16	stench	smell	drain	flower	soap
17	join	ear	win	connect	lose
18	push	bend	stretch	curve	shrink
19	compass	rubber	pen	ruler	pencil
20	need	enjoy	bake	dislike	require

Total

Test 34: Mixed

Test time: 0 5 10 minutes

Look at the first group of three words. The word in the middle has been made from the other two words. Complete the second group of three words in the same way, making a new word in the middle.

Example	PA<u>IN</u>	INTO	<u>TO</u>OK	ALSO	SOON	ONLY
1	PAWN	PALE	RULE	WEST	________	DENT
2	FEEL	FLIP	DRIP	DOOR	________	CRAB
3	WARN	WADE	TIDE	FACE	________	CAME
4	SALT	SOME	OMEN	EVEN	________	ACHE
5	BOTH	KNOT	KNEW	BATH	________	FLOP

Choose the word or phrase that makes each sentence true.

Example A LIBRARY always has (posters, a carpet, <u>books</u>, DVDs, stairs).

6 A HOTEL always has (restaurants, elevators, bedrooms, air conditioning, a garden).

7 A PEN always has (a lid, a case, ink, a cartridge, a book).

8 A FACE always has (a smile, freckles, glasses, a nose, make up).

9 A RABBIT always has (carrots, a hutch, an owner, long ears, spots).

Here is a plan of a recycling area. From the information below, work out what is recycled in each bin.
Here is a list of the things that are recycled:

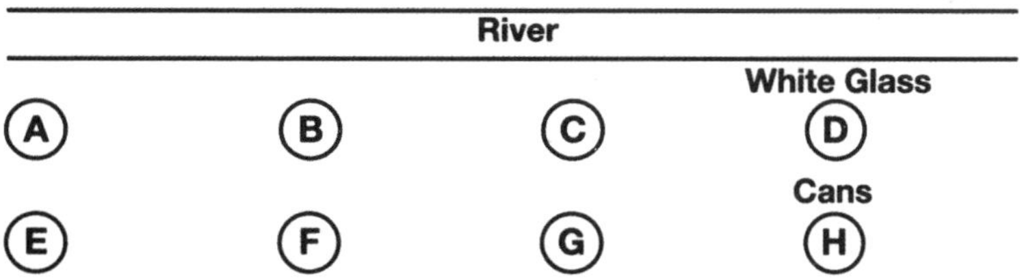

Card is between plastics and shoes and opposite to brown glass.
The glass containers are next to each other by the river.
Green glass is the middle glass container and is not opposite the shoes' bin.

10–15 card ______ shoes ______ plastics ______
green glass ______ brown glass ______ newspapers ______

Find a word that is similar to the word in capital letters and that rhymes with the second word.

Example CABLE tyre wire

16 DRAW fetch ________ **17** CHICKENS towel ________

18 FAST sick ________ **19** PALE spite ________

20 LAW tool ________

Total

Test 35: Mixed

Test time: 0 5 10 minutes

Fill in the crosswords so that all the given words are included. You have been given one letter as a clue in each crossword.

1–3

SUNNY PATHS
HONEY PITCH
TOKEN

	■		■	
	■		■	
	■		■	
	U			

4–6

PARCH KITES
POKER ROTOR
HOSTS

O	■		■	
	■		■	
	■		■	

Underline the one word in the brackets which will go equally well with both the pairs of words outside the brackets.

Example rush, attack cost, fee (price, hasten, strike, charge, money)

7 give, award show, exhibit (welcome, card, tell, present, gift)
8 jelly, preserves push, squeeze (butter, jam, stick, stuff, pack)
9 intelligent, sharp fast, rapid (swift, prompt, clever, blunt, quick)
10 fine, healthy hole, water (fit, drain, pond, well, right)

Remove one letter from the word in capital letters to leave a new word. The meaning of the new word is given in the clue.

Example AUNT an insect ANT

11 CLIMB leg ________
12 BUOY purchase ________
13 PEARL fruit ________
14 SPARK public garden ________

Fill in the missing letters and numbers. The alphabet has been written out to help you.

A B C D E F G H I J K L M N O P Q R S T U V W X Y Z

Example AB is to CD as PQ is to RS.

15 TS is to RQ as PO is to ____.
16 Dw is to Ev as Fu is to ____.
17 3XV is to 4WU as 2TR is to ____.
18 FH is to JL as NP is to ____.
19 P11 is to Q9 as R7 is to ____.
20 NL is to JH as MK is to ____.

Total

Test 36: Mixed

Test time: 0 5 10 minutes

Give the missing numbers and letters in the following sequences.

Example	5	21	8	17	11	13	14	9
1	S5	R3	S7	R4	S9	R5	___	R6
2	7	12	8	___	9	16	10	18
3	12	11	10	10	8	___	6	8
4	___	z	32	y	24	x	16	w
5	V3	2k	W6	2k	___	2k	Y12	2k

Find the missing number by using the two numbers outside the brackets in the same way as the other sets of numbers.

Example 2 [8] 4 3 [18] 6 5 [25] 5

6	6 [3] 3	5 [1] 4	9 [__] 1
7	12 [4] 3	12 [2] 6	12 [__] 12
8	5 [11] 4	3 [12] 7	5 [__] 3
9	10 [4] 2	6 [1] 3	15 [__] 5

Solve the problems by working out the letter codes. The alphabet has been written out to help you.

A B C D E F G H I J K L M N O P Q R S T U V W X Y Z

Example In a code, SECOND is written as UGEQPF. Decode VJKTF. THIRD

10 In a code, SPACE is written as URCEG. Decode ETCD. ______

11 In a code, STEEP is written as QRCCN. Decode UGJJ. ______

12 In a code, SLOPE is written as QJMNC. Decode NMJC. ______

13 In a code, PHONE is written as OGNMD. Decode ONRS. ______

14 In a code, PLANE is written as RNCPG. Decode NQQR. ______

15 In a code, DRAIN is written as ESBJO. Decode GJMF. ______

Underline one word in the brackets which is most opposite in meaning to the word in capitals.

Example WIDE (broad vague long <u>narrow</u> motorway)

16	DEAD	(lifeless	alive	working	gone	arrive)
17	CHEAP	(chick	low	high	expensive	money)
18	HOLD	(twist	hug	release	contain	grip)
19	BRISK	(active	breezy	sluggish	snail	quick)
20	PLAIN	(modest	clear	colour	patterned	frank)

Total

Test 37: Mixed

Test time: 0 5 10 minutes

Here are four number codes: 5793 1375 9375 1379.
Match them to the four words below.

1 DARE ________ 2 BEAR ________

3 READ ________ 4 BEAD ________

Using the same code, decode:

5 19375 ________

Complete the following sentence in the best way by choosing one word from each set of brackets.

Example Tall is to (tree, short, colour) as narrow is to (thin, white, wide).

6 Sheep is to (lamb, wool, hooves) as dog is to (kennel, paws, bark).

7 Bat is to (cricket, tennis, rugby) as stick is to (football, hockey, swimming).

8 Complicated is to (soft, difficult, intelligent) as simple is to (nasty, tricky, easy).

9 Slack is to (hard, loose, strict) as taut is to (rope, tight, tied).

10 Throw is to (catch, fetch, hurl) as cast is to (toss, play, count).

11 Exit is to (hole, entrance, door) as departure is to (arrival, airport, customs).

12–15 Look at these groups of words.

A	B	C	D
India	red	socks	train
England	black	shorts	car
America	green	trousers	bicycle

Choose the correct group for each of the words below. Write in the letter.

Spain ________ shirt ________ yellow ________
orange ________ hat ________ van ________
Norway ________ bus ________

Underline the word in brackets closest in meaning to the word in capitals.

Example UNHAPPY (unkind death laughter sad friendly)

16 RECOVER (bend send lend mend tend)
17 CARING (mother kiss sore tender temper)
18 WORTH (bill time value add money)
19 EMPTY (filled hollow heavy bursting flooded)
20 UNAWARE (ignorant aware beware mind awful)

Total

Test 38: Mixed

Test time: 0 5 10 minutes

In each line underline the word which would come in the middle if the words were arranged in alphabetical order. The alphabet has been written out to help you.

A B C D E F G H I J K L M N O P Q R S T U V W X Y Z

1	hinge	higher	hello	harder	house
2	stork	stone	story	storm	stool
3	patrol	pattern	pathos	paths	patch
4	frame	fringe	frown	front	frost
5	torch	touch	teach	tooth	train

Underline the one word which can be made from the letters of the word in capital letters.

Example CHAMPION camping notch peach cramp <u>chimp</u>

6	FAMOUSLY	mouse	yours	flame	flour	mauls
7	BASKET	token	bathe	skate	tasty	fable
8	ANOTHER	thorny	train	hotter	throne	notes
9	BIRTHDAY	youth	braid	bathe	death	hardly
10	GARDENS	snare	green	snore	drain	sender

Move one letter from the first word and add it to the second word to make two new words.

Example hunt sip hut snip

11	flan	sea	______	______
12	year	brain	______	______
13	snore	bed	______	______
14	heath	torn	______	______

Give the missing letters and numbers in the following sequences. The alphabet has been written out to help you.

A B C D E F G H I J K L M N O P Q R S T U V W X Y Z

Example CQ DP EQ FP GQ <u>HP</u>

15	KL	JL	IM	HM	____	FN
16	Z3	Y5	Z7	Y9	____	Y13
17	____	Hq	Ip	Jo	Kn	Lm
18	FG	IH	____	ML	NO	QP
19	UJ	____	WH	XG	YF	ZE
20	MO	ON	QM	____	UK	WJ

Total

Test 39: Mixed

Test time: 0 5 10 minutes

Underline the pair of words most similar in meaning.

Example come, go roam, wander fear, fare

1	bizarre, weird	perfect, misshapen	green, grass
2	appreciate, ignore	prize, value	effort, laziness
3	out, in	beside, underneath	near, by
4	precious, valuable	priceless, worthless	costly, cheap
5	rags, riches	tatters, shreds	scraps, cloth

Change the first word into the last word by changing one letter at a time and making a new, different word in the middle.

Example CASE CASH LASH

6	DOTE	______________	DARE
7	COAT	______________	BEAT
8	CAST	______________	CURT
9	RAIN	______________	PAIR

If A = 12, B = 10, C = 6, D = 5 and E = 2, find the answers to the following calculations. Give the answer to each calculation as a letter.

10 $\frac{A}{C} =$ ____ **11** $(A - B) \times D =$ ____

12 $D \times E =$ ____ **13** $(C \times E) - B =$ ____

Read the statements and then underline two of the five options that must be true given the information.

14–15 'The Atlantic is an ocean. Oceans surround the lands of the world.'

There are four oceans in the world.
The Atlantic is one of the world's oceans.
Oceans are large bodies of water.
There are oceans in the world.
Whales live in the Atlantic Ocean.

Solve the problems by working out the codes.

16 If & * \ / stands for WING, & * / stands for ______________.

17 If < % ! ? stands for WAIT, < ! ? stands for ______________.

18 If + x x ~ stands for PEEK, ~ x x + stands for ______________.

19 If $ * / ^ stands for MOAT, / ^ * $ stands for ______________.

20 If > ; ; < stands for TOOL, < ; > stands for ______________.

Total

TEST 40: Mixed

Test time: 0 5 10 minutes

If the letters of the alphabet are coded as A = 1, B = 2, C = 3 and so on, what words would these codes make?

1 8945 ____________ 2 6554 ____________

Encode these words using the same code as above.

3 DICE ____________
4 CAGED ____________
5 DEAF ____________

Change one word so that the sentence makes sense. Underline the word you are taking out and write your new word on the line.

Example I waited in line to buy a <u>book</u> to see the film. ticket

6 Here is a plate to spread the jam on your toast. ____________
7 The flash of thunder lit up the night sky. ____________
8 The sheepdog guided the flock of seagulls down the hillside. ____________
9 As a family we recycle bottles, cans, cardboard and newsagent. ____________
10 A policeman helped the old car cross the road and carried his shopping bags for him. ____________
11 As the traffic lights turned to red, the cars started to move forwards. ____________

Four dogs were judged at a dog show out of a total of twenty marks.

The Beagle scored half marks.
The Alsatian only lost 4 marks out of 20.
The Dalmatian got 5 more marks than the Beagle but 3 less than the Collie.

12 How many marks did the Dalmatian receive? ____________
13 Which dog won the competition? ____________
14 How many marks did the Beagle receive? ____________
15 Which dog did better than the Beagle, but not as well as the Alsatian? ____________

Underline the two words which are the odd ones out in the following groups of words.

Example black <u>king</u> purple green <u>house</u>

16	run	pet	crawl	baby	walk
17	quick	rapid	fast	slow	kind
18	remove	blanket	cover	spread	carry
19	cage	frame	coop	crayon	pen
20	friendly	rude	cheerful	scowling	pleasant

Time for a break! Go to Puzzle Page 46

Total

Puzzle 1

Help to build a bridge across the crocodile infested river. Use the word boxes at the bottom of the page to make words that link together – the last two letters of the first word make the first two letters of the next word.

The first word has been placed for you.

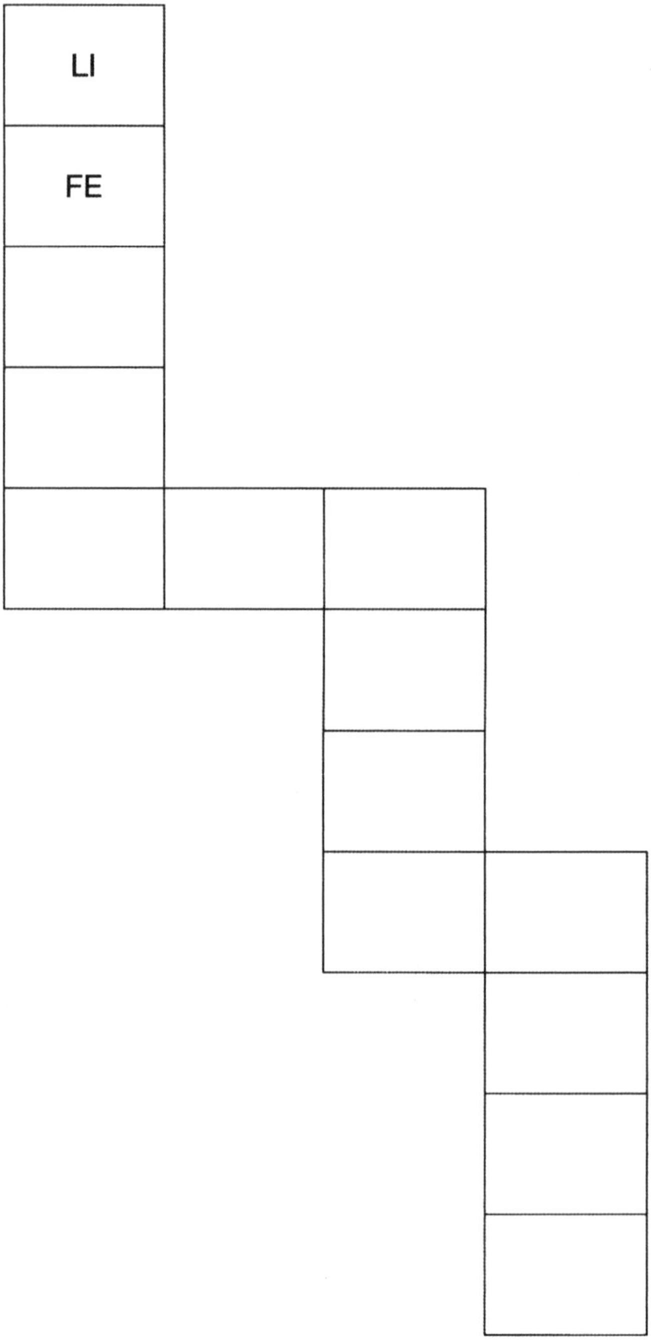

AL	SE
ST	NE
RE	UN
TO	IN
EL	OK
TO	SO

Puzzle 2

Start at the top of the pile of bricks and, working through the layers, make new words by combining two words, one from one layer and the other from the layer below it.

You must go down each time, not sideways.

Here is an example:

BLACK
OUT | BERRY
DOOR

Both BLACKOUT and BLACKBERRY are new words, but only

OUTDOOR makes sense as the next word.

Now try these. Be careful, there is only one path through!

CAMP
ROUND | FIRE
WATER | WORK | PLACE
HEEL | SHOP | OUT | MAT
CHAIR | FRONT | SIDE | DOOR | TIN
TABLE | WAYS | MAN | STOP
CLOTH | AGE | KIND
LESS | HEARTED
ON

TURN
OVER | NIP
HAND | GROWN | PER
SOME | FULL | UP | FORM
HOW | TIME | LOAD | ALL | LESS
EVER | SHARE | RIGHT | ROUND
GREEN | HOLDER | WING
HOUSE | MIRROR
WIFE

Puzzle ❸

Sarah is tired and wants to go home.

There are several routes that will take her home, but her mother wants her to use a specific one. She has given Sarah written instructions to follow.

Unfortunately, Sarah's older brother has placed three other sets of instructions in Sarah's backpack. Which is the correct set of instructions to take her back home?

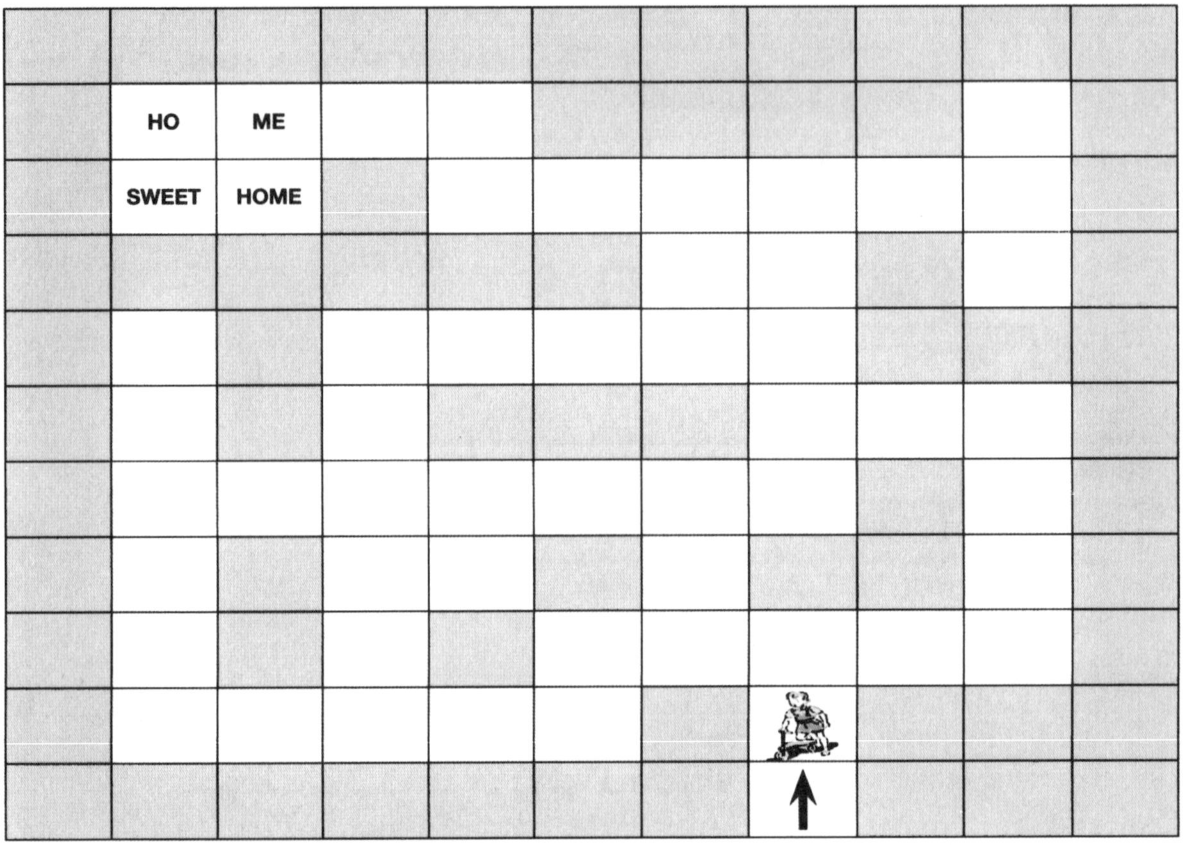

The letters show the compass directions (north, south, east, west). The numbers show the number of squares Sarah should travel (for example, N1 means go north, 1 square).

Here are the four sets of instructions:

A	**B**	**C**	**D**
N1	N1	N1	N1
W1	W2	E2	W1
N2	S1	N3	N2
W3	W4	W2	E1
N2	N3	N3	N4
E4	E2	W3	E2
S2	N2	N1	N1
W4	W1	W2	W1

Puzzle 4

In the centre of each flower is a word. Write a word on each of the petals that can be made using the letters of the centre word. You may only use each letter once. Each word must be three or more letters long.

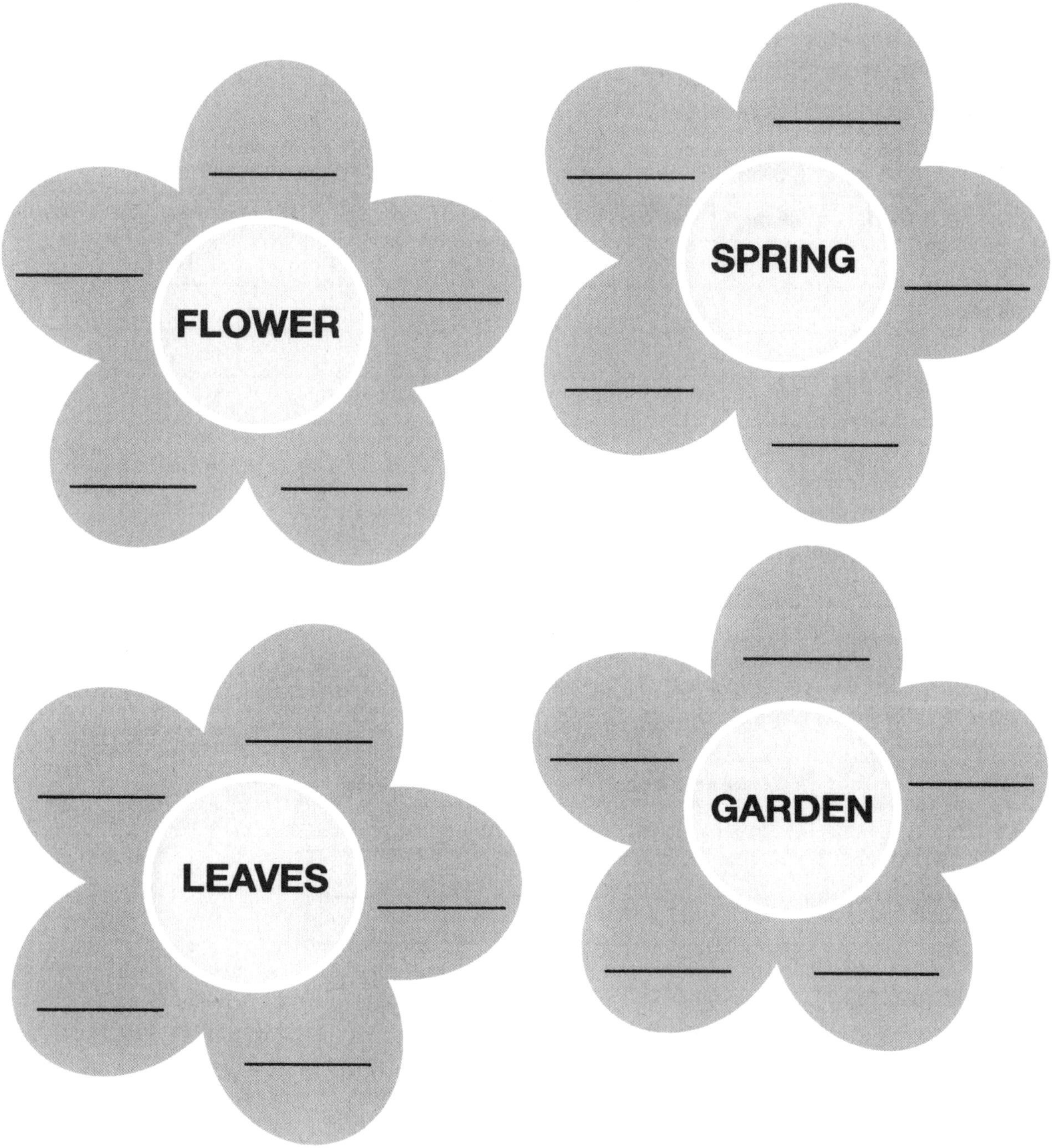

Puzzle 5

Mia, Nathan, Rohan and Sita played a game of dice. Each of them had a pair of different coloured dice – red, blue, yellow or green. The idea of the game was to throw as many sixes as they could in 20 throws. They ended up throwing 5, 7, 12 and 14 sixes.

Using the grid and clues below, work out which colour dice each child had and how many sixes he or she threw.

The first clue has been done for you.

	Colour of dice					Number of sixes			
	Red	**Blue**	**Yellow**	**Green**		**5**	**7**	**12**	**14**
Mia			✗	✗				✔	
Nathan									
Rohan									
Sita									

Clues:

1 Mia scored 12 sixes. Mia does not have yellow or green dice.

2 Nathan has yellow dice.

3 Rohan has blue dice but has not thrown 7 sixes.

4 The child with the green dice has the lowest score.

Your grid should now be complete. Fill in the table below to show the number of sixes each child scored and their dice colour.

Children	**Colour of dice**	**Number of sixes**
Mia		
Nathan		
Rohan		
Sita		

Progress Grid

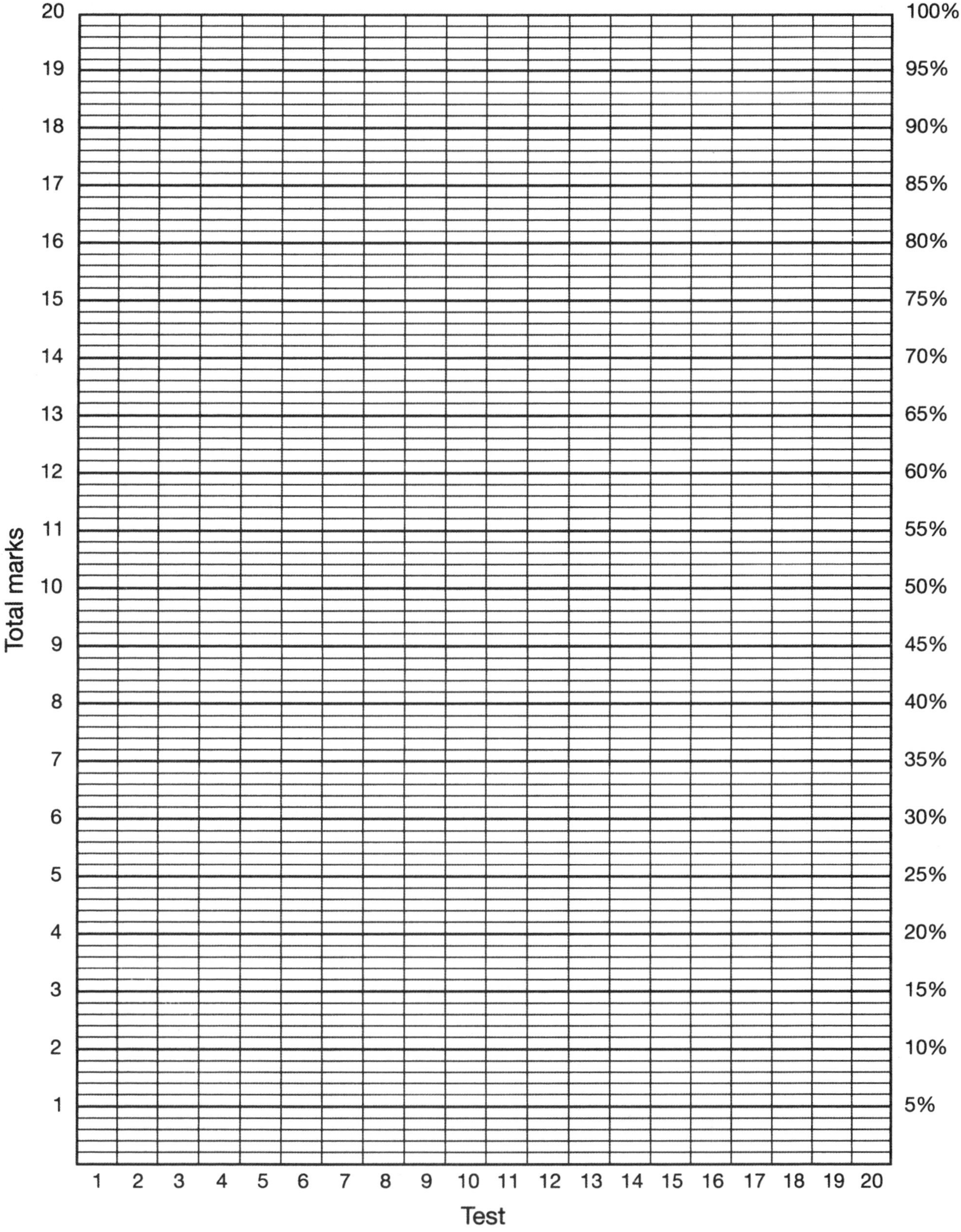

Progress Grid

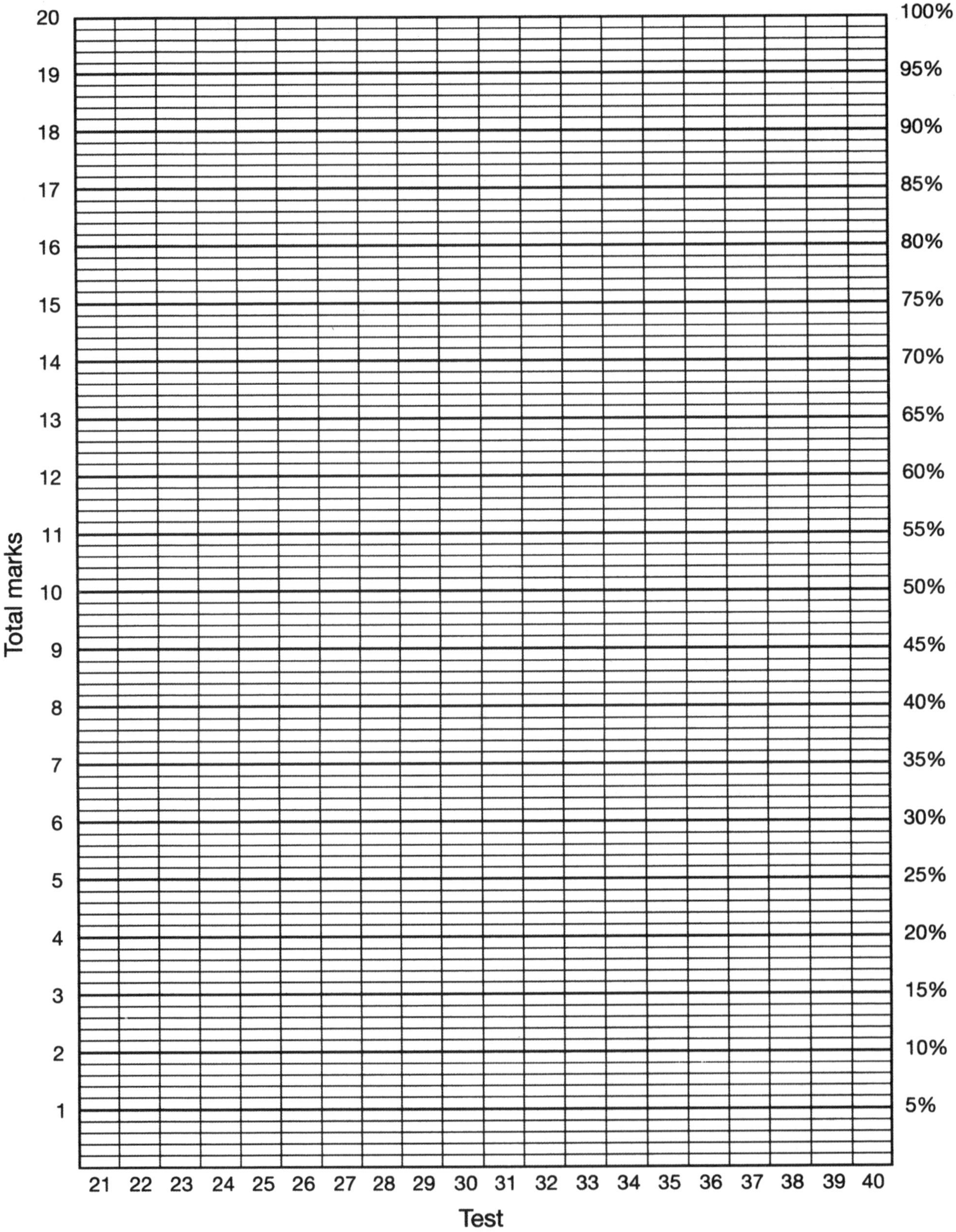